D1470235

WORLD MYTHOLOGIES

MYTHS OF THE ANCIENT EGYPTIANS

Patricia Dawson

Cavendish Square

New York

Published in 2016 by Cavendish Square Publishing, LLC
243 5th Avenue, Suite 136, New York, NY 10016

Website: cavendishsq.com

This publication represents the opinions and views of the author based on his or her personal experience, knowledge, and research. The information in this book serves as a general guide only. The author and publisher have used their best efforts in preparing this book and disclaim liability rising directly or indirectly from the use and application of this book.

CPSIA Compliance Information: Batch #CW16CSQ

All websites were available and accurate when this book was sent to press.

Library of Congress Cataloging-in-Publication Data

Dawson, Patricia (Patricia Adelaide), author.
Myths of the ancient Egyptians / Patricia Dawson.
pages cm. — (World mythologies)
ISBN 978-1-5026-0986-1 (hardcover) ISBN 978-1-5026-0987-8 (ebook)
1. Mythology, Egyptian. 2. Gods, Egyptian. 3. Egypt—Religion. I. Title. II. Series: World mythologies.
BL2441.3.D39 2016
299'.3113—dc23
2015023863

Editorial Director: David McNamara
Editor: Amy Hayes
Copy Editor: Rebecca Rohan
Art Director: Jeffrey Talbot
Designer: Joseph Macri
Senior Production Manager: Jennifer Ryder-Talbot
Production Editor: Renni Johnson
Photo Research: J8 Media

The photographs in this book are used by permission and through the courtesy of: Leoks/Shutterstock.com, cover; Pius Lee/Shutterstock.com, 4; Goodall, Frederick/Private Collection/Christie's Images/Bridgeman Images, 8-9; Scarpelli, Tancredi/Private Collection/Look and Learn/Bridgeman Images, 10; Valley of the Queens, Thebes, Egypt/Bridgeman Images, 14; Jackson, Peter/Private Collection/Look and Learn/Peter Jackson Collection/Bridgeman Images, 18; Universal History Archive/Getty Images, 21; Steven G. Johnson/Thoth-baboon-British-Museum.jpg/Wikimedia Commons, 23; De Agostini Picture Library/Getty Images, 25; Dea/G. Dagli ORTI/De Agostini/Getty Images, 28-29; DeAgostini/Getty Images, 30; Werner Forman/Universal Images Group/Getty Images, 35; Public Domain/http://mail.wikipedia.org/pipermail/wikide-l/2005-April/012195.html/Ägyptischer Maler um 1360 v. Chr. 001.jpg/Wikimedia Commons, 36; De Agostini Picture Library/G. Dagli Orti/Bridgeman Images, 38; Werner Forman Archive/Bridgeman Images, 41; Champollion, Jean Francois/Private Collection/Archives Charmet/Bridgeman Images, 43; Jose Ignacio Soto/Shutterstock.com, 47; Dea/G. Dagli Orti/De Agostini/Getty Images, 48; Prisma/UIG via Getty Images, 52; DeAgostini/W. Buss/Getty Images, 58; CM Dixon/Print Collector/Getty Images, 61; Wolfgang Kaehler/LightRocket via Getty Images, 63; Alain Guileux/Age Fotostock, 66; Brooklyn Museum/ Head of the God Osiris, ca. 595-525 B.C.E..jpg/Wikimedia Commons, 74; CM Dixon/Print Collector/Getty Images, 76; CM Dixon/Print Collector/Getty Images, 80; Abydos Tempelrelief Ramses II.jpg/Wikimedia Commons, 83.

Printed in the United States of America

TABLE OF CONTENTS

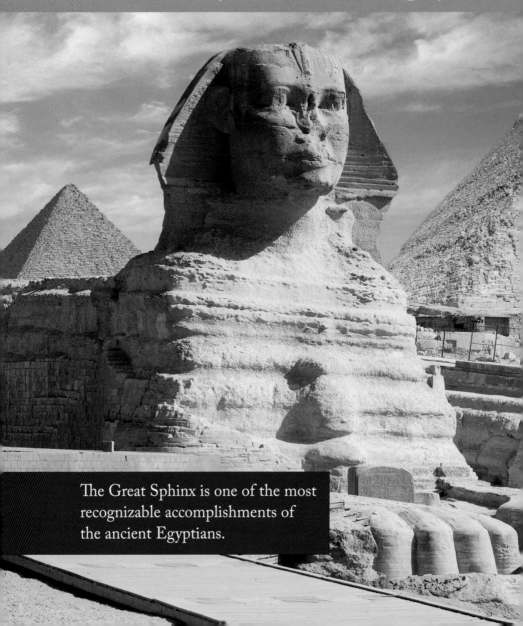

The Importance of Mythology

The Great Sphinx is one of the most recognizable accomplishments of the ancient Egyptians.

From folk heroes to gods, campfires to cathedrals, myths are stories that told over and over again. These important stories deepen the identity and customs of a culture. Myths shaped the lives of the people who heard them. These timeless tales of a civilization's gods and heroes were a part of the beliefs, values, and practices of people who lived long ago.

What makes a story a myth? Unlike a narrative written by a particular author, a myth is a traditional story that has been handed down from generation to generation, first orally and later in written form. Nearly all myths tell the deeds of gods, goddesses, and other divine beings. These age-old tales were once widely accepted as true and sacred. Their primary purpose was to explain the mysteries of life and the origins of a society's customs, institutions, and religious rituals.

Mythology (the whole collection of myths belonging to a society) played an important role in ancient cultures. In very early times, people created myths to explain the awe-inspiring, uncontrollable forces of nature, such as thunder, lightning, darkness, drought, and death. Even after philosophers and scientists began to develop more rational explanations for these mysteries, myths continued to provide comforting answers to the many questions that could never be fully resolved. People of all cultures have asked the same basic questions about the world around them, such as how did the world begin, what is the purpose of living, and what happens after death?

The myths of ancient Egypt are exciting, heartbreaking, and bloody. There is trickery, wisdom, and sacrifice. These myths were not just created out of people's imaginations. A civilization's geography, government, and culture all influence what stories are told, and which stories eventually become myth. For example, while most cultures have a myth of a great flood, Egypt's tale of nature trying to kill off humanity is about the sun. This is because the Egyptian floods were essential for a good harvest, while the harsh, hot desert was to be feared and respected.

Mythology serves as instruction, inspiration, and entertainment. Well-known stories offer people in a society a way to express their fundamental beliefs and values and communicate these beliefs to future generations. Myths preserve and embellish tales of a civilization's accomplishments and teach important lessons about conduct and priorities. These captivating stories provided enjoyment to countless listeners and readers in ancient times, just as they do today.

Pronouncing Egyptian Names

There is no "correct" way to spell or pronounce the names of the Egyptian gods and goddesses. No one has spoken ancient Egyptian in more than 1,500 years. The people of Egypt wrote their words without vowels, in a system of pictures and symbols known as **hieroglyphs**. That makes it even harder for modern-day scholars to write the language and figure out how it sounded. For the spellings and pronunciation guides in this book, we have tried to use the most familiar and easy-to-say forms of names. If you think that something should be pronounced another way, go ahead and try it. You may be right!

MYTHS OF THE
ANCIENT
EGYPTIANS

PART 1:
Who Were the Egyptians?

The Floods of the Nile

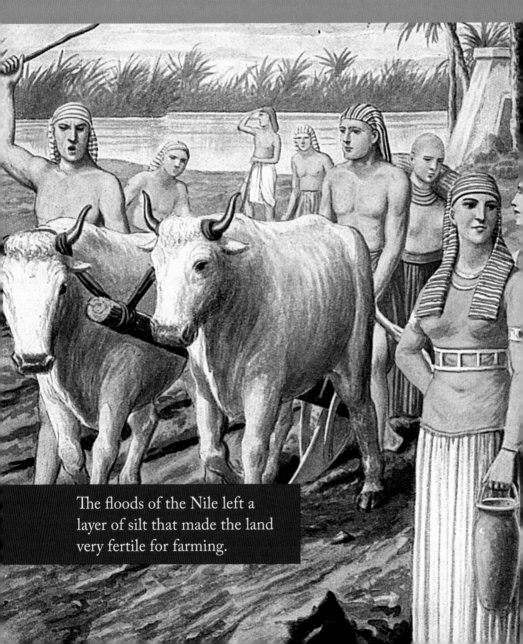

The floods of the Nile left a layer of silt that made the land very fertile for farming.

Egypt, in northeast Africa, was a land of extreme weather. There was either drought or floods. The vast majority of Egypt was desert. However, life thrived around the Nile River, the main water source for the entire civilization.

The Nile River, the longest river in the world, flowed south to north through the center of these vast dry wastelands. Each spring, the Nile would swell with rain and melting snow from the mountains of Ethiopia, far to the south. Around the end of June, the waters reached Egypt and the Nile would overflow, flooding the river valley. When the waters slowly receded, they would leave behind a layer of rich black **silt** that was perfect for planting crops. Ancient Egypt grew up on the long narrow strip of fertile land that bordered the life-giving Nile. The Egyptians called their homeland Kemet, or "Black Land," after the dark soil that made their civilization possible.

The annual **inundation**, or flood of the Nile, inspired many of ancient Egypt's myths. In the creation story retold on page 30, the world rises from the **Primeval** (original) Waters, just as Kemet emerged from the receding floodwaters. Some years the Nile failed to flood, leading to drought and famine, while other years brought too much water, wiping out entire communities. The story of "Ra's Wrath" on page 38, in which the gods punish humankind for their sins, may have developed to explain natural disasters such as these.

Despite the environmental uncertainties of their home, the ancient Egyptians regarded the inundation as proof that there was an order in the universe. This order, known as ***maat,*** was set in place and maintained by the gods. In maat, Egypt was the center of all creation. The deserts and foreign lands beyond the Nile Valley were part of the realm of chaos, which constantly threatened the divine order.

Egyptians who needed to discuss maat often used metaphors and stories. In these stories, which became the foundation of Egyptian religion and myth, maat was often embodied and personified by a goddess wearing an ostrich feather on her head. As discussed in "Judgment in the Afterlife" on page 74, Maat's feather was used to judge the souls of the dead.

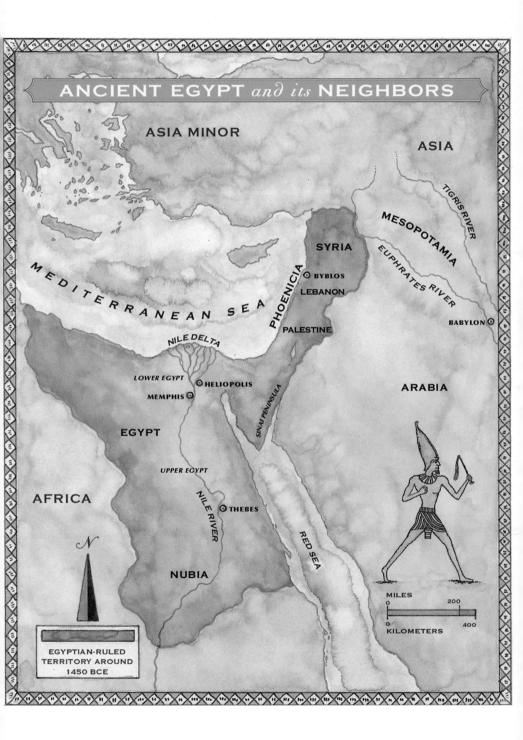

ANCIENT EGYPT *and its* NEIGHBORS

ASIA MINOR

ASIA

TIGRIS RIVER

MESOPOTAMIA

EUPHRATES RIVER

SYRIA

○ BYBLOS

LEBANON

BABYLON ○

M E D I T E R R A N E A N   S E A

PHOENICIA

PALESTINE

NILE DELTA

LOWER EGYPT

○ HELIOPOLIS

MEMPHIS ○

ARABIA

SINAI PENINSULA

EGYPT

UPPER EGYPT

AFRICA

NILE RIVER

○ THEBES

RED SEA

N

NUBIA

MILES
0   200

0   400
KILOMETERS

EGYPTIAN-RULED
TERRITORY AROUND
1450 BCE

The Kingdoms of Egypt

This is a portrait of Ramesses III, a king who ruled during the twentieth dynasty.

The Black Land was divided into two kingdoms. Upper Egypt lay to the south, while Lower Egypt lay to the north. It might seem strange to look at a traditional northern-oriented map and see that Upper Egypt is actually below Lower Egypt. However, the Egyptians oriented themselves according to the flow of the Nile. The Nile flowed south to north, and so the Egyptians considered southern lands up, the northern lands down, or low.

For many years these two kingdoms were separate. However, around 3100 BCE, a legendary king known as Menes united the two lands into one large nation-state. That unification marked the beginning of the ancient Egyptian civilization.

The ancient Egyptians organized their history by dynasties. Dynasties were powerful families who passed down their rule from generation to generation. The history of Egypt's thirty dynasties spans nearly three thousand years. Modern-day historians break that long stretch of time into several shorter periods. See page 16 for one commonly accepted outline of Egyptian history.

The Dynasties of Egypt

Early Dynasties circa 3100–2680 BCE
Dynasties 1–2

The first kings establish Egypt's capital at Memphis. The system of pictures and symbols known as hieroglyphs develops into the state's first written language.

Old Kingdom circa 2680–2180 BCE
Dynasties 3–6

Powerful kings build the first pyramids. Sculptors and tomb painters create some of the greatest art in Egypt's history. The Pyramid Texts date from this period.

First Intermediate Period circa 2180–2050 BCE
Dynasties 7–10

Rival dynasties war over control of the state. A king of the southern city of Thebes eventually reunites Egypt.

Middle Kingdom circa 2050–1800 BCE
Dynasties 11–12

Strong kings expand trade and conquer Nubia, a region to the south. The Coffin Texts date from this period.

Second Intermediate Period circa 1800–1550 BCE
Dynasties 13–17

The Hyksos, invaders from western Asia, set up a rival dynasty in northern Egypt. In time they are expelled, and Egypt is reunited.

New Kingdom circa 1550–1085 BCE
Dynasties 18–20

Powerful warrior-kings establish a great empire stretching all the way from Nubia to the Euphrates River in Syria. Toward the end of the New Kingdom, foreign invaders begin to chip away at the empire. The Book of the Dead dates from this period.

Third Intermediate Period circa 1085–747 BCE
Dynasties 21–24

Egypt's government becomes increasingly weak and divided. Dynasties of Libyan origin rule in the north, while priests govern in the southern capital of Thebes.

Late Period circa 747–332 BCE
Dynasties 25–30

Egypt is invaded and occupied by foreign powers, including the Nubians, the Assyrians, and the Persians. The threats to Egypt's traditional culture inspire scholars to record many of the ancient myths that have been passed down orally from generation to generation. In 332 BCE the Greek armies of Alexander the Great conquer Egypt.

The crowning of Alexander the Great as king of Egypt put an end to the long line of dynasties. After Alexander's death, Egypt came under the control of one of his generals, Ptolemy I. Worship of the ancient Egyptian deities continued under Ptolemy's successors, who ruled the state for the next three hundred years.

In 30 BCE, Roman forces defeated the last Ptolemaic ruler, Cleopatra VII. Egypt became a part of the Roman Empire and eventually adopted Christianity. The ancient gods and goddesses faded from religious icons to myths. Then, in 640 CE, Islam was brought over by invaders from the Arabian Peninsula, beginning a fresh chapter in Egyptian history.

Society's Pyramid

The Great Pyramid of Giza was constructed by many slaves and common people for the pleasure of a single king. It is a perfect metaphor for the social structure of ancient Egypt.

E gypt is known for its stunning stone pyramids, constructed thousands of years ago. However, these were not the only pyramids of Egypt. Ancient Egyptian society was like a pyramid, with many people in the lowest class, and one supreme ruler at the top.

At the base of this society pyramid was the great mass of common people. Most commoners worked the land, raising crops and livestock. From time to time, they might be required to labor on pyramids, temples, and other state building projects.

The Egyptian middle class consisted mainly of merchants, skilled craftsmen, and educated people such as doctors, teachers, and engineers. The upper class included high-ranking government officials, priests, military officers, **scribes**, and nobles. While ordinary farmers lived in simple mud-brick huts, the richest and most powerful nobles owned luxurious town houses and sprawling country estates. They had laborers to work their fields and servants who attended to their every need.

At the very top of the social pyramid was the king or **pharaoh**. (The title pharaoh, meaning "great house," was adopted by kings during the New Kingdom period.) From very early times, Egypt's kings were regarded as earthly gods, part human and part divine. The king was a link between heaven and earth. His reign ensured the gods' blessings on his subjects and maintained the divine order of the universe. In addition to these awesome responsibilities, he was the head of the government, the courts, and the military.

A large and complicated bureaucracy helped the king fulfill his many obligations. Members of the government included a chief minister called the **vizier** (vuh-ZEER) and other court officials. Governors and administrators oversaw day-to-day affairs in Egypt's numerous provinces, or "nomes." A host of priests acted on the king's behalf in temples throughout the country.

Women did not serve in the government. Their primary role was to have children and manage their households. However, Egyptian women did enjoy more rights than women in most other parts of the ancient world. They could own property, borrow money, run their own businesses, and move about freely in public. Although husbands were the head of the household, wives enjoyed considerable respect and authority within their homes.

While women were not allowed to serve in government, Egyptian queens could wield great power. A few of these queens even rose to the title of pharoah. Hatshepsut, for example, became one of the most famous leaders of Egypt.

A Large Family of Gods

Thoth was one of the most important gods of Egyptian mythology. He was sometimes depicted with the head of an ibis, a bird with a long, thin beak.

Before Egypt was an empire, every Egyptian town and village worshipped its own gods. After government was unified under the kings, many of these earlier, local deities did not disappear. Instead, they became part of an enormous "extended family" of gods and goddesses.

This extended family continued to develop over the course of nearly three thousand years. Some gods merged into one another. Some took on new characteristics. New gods were borrowed from other cultures. The result was a rich, many-sided religion embracing hundreds of deities and many complex, often contradictory, beliefs.

The ancient Egyptians believed that their gods created the world and were involved in every area of life. A number of deities were living forms of natural forces. There were gods of the sun, the moon, the earth, the sky, storms, and the inundation. Other deities represented aspects of life, such as war, wisdom, justice, healing, and childbirth. The stories that were told about all these gods and goddesses helped the Egyptians explain the many mysteries of the world around them. The family tree shows some of the most important gods and goddesses, along with their most common roles.

An Egyptian god might take several human, part-human, and animal forms. For example, Thoth was the god of the moon as well as knowledge and writing. He was often pictured as a man with the head of an ibis (a stork-like bird) but also could be represented entirely as an ibis or as a baboon.

This quartzite sculpture is a depiction of Thoth as a baboon. Each god could have many different forms that represented them.

Gods died and were reborn many times in Egyptian mythology. The Egyptians believed in life after death not only for gods, but for people too. Spirits of dead mortals who had lived righteous lives were welcomed into a divine domain ruled by Osiris, god of the dead. "The Dying God Osiris" on page 48, tells the story of how this important god became king of the Afterworld.

FAMILY TREE *of the* ANCIENT EGYPTIAN GODS

The ancient Egyptians worshipped hundreds of different gods and goddesses. Here are a few of the most important deities, with their special areas of responsibility.

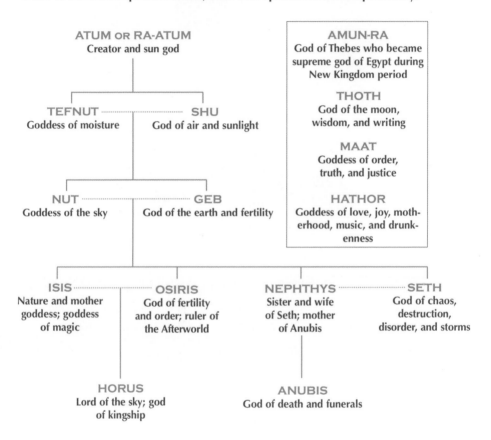

ATUM OR RA-ATUM
Creator and sun god

TEFNUT
Goddess of moisture

SHU
God of air and sunlight

NUT
Goddess of the sky

GEB
God of the earth and fertility

AMUN-RA
God of Thebes who became supreme god of Egypt during New Kingdom period

THOTH
God of the moon, wisdom, and writing

MAAT
Goddess of order, truth, and justice

HATHOR
Goddess of love, joy, motherhood, music, and drunkenness

ISIS
Nature and mother goddess; goddess of magic

OSIRIS
God of fertility and order; ruler of the Afterworld

NEPHTHYS
Sister and wife of Seth; mother of Anubis

SETH
God of chaos, destruction, disorder, and storms

HORUS
Lord of the sky; god of kingship

ANUBIS
God of death and funerals

Gods: Rulers of Life and Death

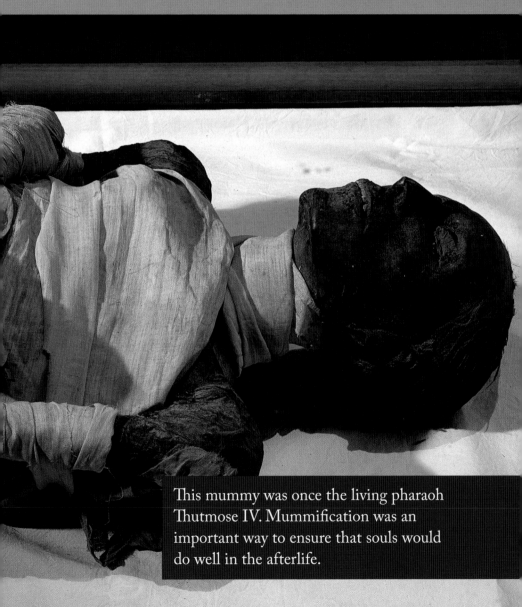

This mummy was once the living pharaoh Thutmose IV. Mummification was an important way to ensure that souls would do well in the afterlife.

Egyptians believed that their gods were a living part of the world. From the pharaoh down to the fieldworker, people did all they could to stay in the favors of these ever-present deities. Religion and ceremony were essential parts of everyday life.

Nearly every major Egyptian deity had its own temple. The temple was regarded as the house of the god. A host of priests performed daily rituals including hymns, prayers, and offerings to ensure that the gods were happy in their earthly homes.

Ordinary people were never admitted into the inner areas of the temple. However, the public did enjoy access to the gods during the annual religious festivals, when the sacred image of the god was carried from the temple shrine through the streets in a grand procession of priests, musicians, dancers, and acrobats. The Egyptians also prayed to their favorite gods at small shrines in their homes. They used private rituals to protect the sick, newborn children, and women going through pregnancy and childbirth. Nearly everyone wore **amulets**, small charms often made in the shape of a god or goddess. These miniature images were believed to grant the wearer divine favor and protection.

The ancient Egyptians' religious beliefs followed them into death. At the center of their funeral practices was the belief that every person had two spiritual forms, the *ba* and the *ka*. After death the ba journeyed to the Afterworld, where it faced judgment before the throne of Osiris. Meanwhile, the ka remained with the body. In order for a person to enjoy eternal life in the Afterworld, his or her body had to be preserved and given a proper burial, with all the essential religious rituals.

The bodies of all but the poorest Egyptians were preserved as mummies. The internal organs were removed, and the body was treated with a special salt called natron for about forty days. Then it was anointed with oils, bandaged in strips of linen, and placed in a coffin. "The Dying God Osiris" (page 48) explains the origins of **mummification** and other ancient Egyptian funeral practices.

Once the bodies were mummified, they were buried in brick or stone tombs. The pyramids built for the kings are the most elaborate examples of these tombs. Some scholars believe that these magnificent monuments represented the Primeval Mound, discussed in the first myth of Part II, "How the World Began."

MYTHS OF THE ANCIENT EGYPTIANS

PART 2:
Stories and Myths

How the World Began

Two of the most powerful gods, Atum and Osiris, sit back to back in this fresco painted on the tomb of Nefertari.

Egyptian myths are shorter stories that are woven together like threads to create a fabric of myths. The first thread of this fabric is the story of the creation of the world. Nearly every major city in Egypt had its own version of the creation story, with a different god as creator. However, the inconsistencies among all these stories did not bother the Egyptians. Their myths were not intended as precise explanations of the way the universe came into being and weren't considered strictly factual. Instead, these ancient stories helped Egyptians express their ideas about life's mysteries.

All of the different creation myths were inspired by the natural world. Observing the annual flood of the Nile, the Egyptians concluded that the earth began as a hill of soil called the Primeval Mound, which rose from an endless ocean of chaos known as the Primeval Waters. Even after creation, the Primeval Waters continued to surround the world. Every Egyptian temple was designed with gateways, columns, and other features representing the moment of creation and the divine forces that preserved the careful balance between the forces of order and chaos.

Our version of the Egyptian creation story comes from the ancient city of Heliopolis, center for the worship of the sun god Atum. In the Heliopolitan myth, Atum emerges from the Primeval Waters and sets about creating the world and all its creatures. The god's children, grandchildren, and great-grandchildren assist him in his task. Egyptian gods and goddesses were often born in pairs, and brothers and sisters might marry and have children.

Fragments of the Heliopolitan creation story have been found in **inscriptions** and writings inside Egyptian temples and tombs. The oldest surviving source is the Pyramid Texts. This collection of spells, charms, hymns, prayers, and other sacred writings dates back to the Old Kingdom period. The ancient texts were carved inside the pyramid tombs of kings and queens to protect their bodies and help their spirits rise to the heavens.

Dramatis Personae

Dramatis Personae is a Latin phrase meaning "persons of the drama," or cast of characters. Here are the gods who play a role in the Egyptian creation story:

Atum (AH-tum) Creator and sun god

Shu (SHOO) God of the air

Tefnut (TEF-noot) Goddess of moisture

Geb (GEB) God of the earth

Nut (NOOT) Goddess of the sky

Osiris (oh-SIE-rus) God of fertility, order, and the dead

Seth (SET) God of chaos, disorder, and storms

Haroeris (har-WER-is) Falcon-winged god

Isis (EYE-sus) Goddess of nature, motherhood, and magic

Nephthys (NEF-this) Sister and wife of Seth

Atum the Creator

In the beginning, all was chaos. An ocean of black swirling waters stretched through the void of space, without shape or form or boundaries. Then, out of the Primeval Waters came Atum, lord of the heavens and earth. Some say that the great god emerged from a shining egg. Others tell us that he arose from a blue lotus flower. Still others declare that Atum created himself out of nothingness simply by uttering his own name. However the wondrous event came to pass, Atum stepped from the waters onto the Primeval Mound, and the first rays of light pierced the timeless darkness.

> The sky had not yet come into being, the earth had not yet come into being, the gods had not yet been born.
>
> ~ Pyramid Texts

For ages Atum sat alone in the universe. In his loneliness he longed for a companion. At last he decided to make the first creatures. He spit, and out popped Shu, god of the air. He spit again, and there stood Tefnut, goddess of the dew and moisture. Joyfully embracing his little ones, the creator gave them his protection and a share of his divine powers.

When Shu and Tefnut grew up, they left their father to wander in the dark waters. In time they became the proud parents of twins named Geb and Nut. Geb was the god of the earth. A lively boy, he had skin as green as emeralds and a booming laugh that shook the darkness like an earthquake. Nut was the goddess of the sky.

Sweet and gentle, she wore a flowing blue gown studded with sparkling stars. Although they were very different, the two children adored each other. In fact, they were so devoted that they could not bear to be

> O Nut! … O Great One who has become the sky!
>
> ~ Pyramid Texts

separated. All day long brother and sister sat nose-to-nose, arms entwined, laughing and whispering together.

Now, Shu was a loving father. He tried to be patient with his children. But the great god Atum had left it up to him to continue the work of creation, and as long as earth and sky were so close, nothing could grow between them. Shu ordered Geb and Nut to stop their foolishness. The pair simply ignored him. Finally, he took matters into his own hands. He lifted up his daughter Nut and held her high above his head. He pressed Geb to the ground, holding his son down with his feet. That is how our world took shape, with the sky above, the earth below, and a space in between filled with the life-giving air. To this day, the dark waters still lurk outside the world's boundaries, held in place by the will of the gods.

Once earth and sky were separated, Shu had room to create plants and trees, rivers and mountains. He made a host of creatures to fill the air, land, and water, from birds and beasts to fish and reptiles. When Atum saw the beauty of the new world, he wept for joy. His golden tears hit the earth and became the first man and woman. Then, at Atum's command, Shu breathed the breath of life into humanity.

As for the twins Geb and Nut, even separation could not put an end to their great love. In time, five children were born from their devotion. Osiris was good and honorable, while Seth loved evil and disorder. Haroeris had wings like a falcon. The sisters of these three gods

Here you can see the twins Geb, the green figure to the left, and Nut, the large goddess who looms over everything. Shu is in the middle holding them apart.

This painting of a goddess with hieroglyphics is in the tomb of Seti I from the Valley of the Kings.

were Isis and Nephthys. Isis would grow up to become the devoted wife of Osiris, and Seth would marry Nephthys. From the union of these two divine couples would come all the descendants of Atum.

At last the gods had created the world. Divine and mortal lived together in the new-made world, with Atum as their ruler. Under his reign the earth would know a golden age.

Why There Are
365 Days in a Year

Like many ancient peoples, the Egyptians based their first calendar on the cycles of the moon. They soon noticed, however, that their 360-day calendar was out of step with the seasons, which change according to the earth's movement around the sun. To solve this problem, they added five days at the end of the calendar year. An ancient Egyptian myth, retold by the Greek historian Plutarch around 100 CE, explained the origin of those special days.

Atum became angry when the union between the sky goddess Nut and the earth god Geb delayed the creation of the world. After the pair was separated, Atum saw that Nut was pregnant. In his wrath he "invoked a curse upon her that she should not give birth to a child in any month or year." But Thoth, god of wisdom, took pity on Nut. The clever god challenged the moon to a game of dice. When Thoth won the game, he claimed a portion of the moon's light as his prize.

From the moon's light, Thoth created five extra days, which he added to the existing year. Because the days did not belong to any month, Nut could use them to give birth to her five children. "The Egyptians even now call these five days intercalated [inserted]," wrote Plutarch, "and celebrate them as the birthdays of the gods."

Ra's Wrath

The sun god Ra was often depicted as a human with a falcon head.

The early Egyptians worshipped Ra, the sun god, as the source of light and energy. Over time, the popularity of Ra transformed him into the primary creator god. Other creator gods were merged with Ra to form new deities, such as Ra-Atum. Ra's supreme power became part of the Egyptian government, as kings began to claim him as their ancestor. Beginning with the Fourth Dynasty, every Egyptian ruler was called the Son of Ra.

In Egyptian myths about the golden age that followed creation, Ra is king of both gods and humans. When the people of the earth begin to plot against him, he must send his Eye, in the form of the goddess Hathor, to teach them a lesson. Unfortunately, Hathor develops an unquenchable thirst for human blood. It is up to Ra to devise a clever plan to save the human race from extinction.

This grisly tale of divine vengeance emphasized the importance of maintaining a proper relationship with the gods. The Egyptian gods were believed to be basically good and merciful, but they were also quick to punish any mortal who offended them through words, deeds, or a lack of devotion. Other ancient peoples told similar stories of divine punishment. However, the Egyptian tale had at least one unique feature. In other lands catastrophe usually came in the form of a great flood. In ancient Egypt, where the annual flood of the Nile was seen as a blessing, the destructive force was the Eye of the sun god instead. The Eye of Ra was a mysterious figure that was capable of separating from the god and venturing out on its own. Like the sun itself, the Eye brought light and life, but its blazing heat could also turn fertile lands into desert wastes.

The myth of Ra's vengeance is found in an ancient religious text known as *The Book of the Divine Cow*. This collection of magic spells was carved in the tombs of pharaohs during the New Kingdom period. The earliest known copy was discovered in the tomb of the Eighteenth Dynasty pharaoh Tutankhamen, often known today as "King Tut."

Dramatis Personae

Ra (RAH) Creator and sun god

Nun (NOON) God of the Primeval Waters

Hathor (HAH-thor) Goddess of love, joy, and drunkenness

Nut (NOOT) Goddess of the sky

Thoth (THOATH or TOAT) God of the moon, wisdom, and writing

The Eye of Ra

In ancient times, when the world was new, gods and humans lived together on earth. Their king was Ra, god of the sun, who dwelt among them in the form of a man. Each day the mighty lord walked forth to inspect his domain. So great was his power that all people showed him reverence, and none dared oppose him. Under the reign of Ra, the world was a paradise where peace, joy, and prosperity flowered.

To the gods the centuries are like years. But as the long ages passed, even Ra began to feel the effects of time on his earthly body. The great god became old and frail. His bones, flesh, and hair changed from divine matter into precious stones and metals. Wicked men began to whisper behind his back. "Behold!" they said. "The king's bones are silver. His skin is pale gold. His beard is as blue as **lapis lazuli**. Why should we obey such a decrepit old ruler?"

Ra heard the men mocking him, and his heart filled with rage. He summoned the gods and goddesses to a secret meeting at his palace. As soon as the council had assembled, he turned to

The Eye of Ra was the goddess Hathor, who took the form of a fierce lioness.

Nun, from whose Primeval Waters the sun god himself had first risen. "Eldest one, give me your counsel," Ra said. "Mankind turns against me. The mortals that I created are plotting to overthrow me. In my heart I desire to punish them, but I will not act until you have spoken."

Nun answered, "Mighty Ra, all men fear the blazing power of your Eye. Send forth the Eye of Ra to slay these evil people." Then all the gods and goddesses raised their voices, urging Ra to follow Nun's wise counsel.

Their advice was just what Ra had been hoping for. Nodding grimly, he plucked out the blazing orb that crowned his forehead. In an instant the Eye of Ra took the form of the god's beloved daughter Hathor. To the people of earth, Hathor was like a mother, adored for her kind and joyful nature. On this day, though, she was filled with her father's fury. As the divine assembly watched in amazement, her beautiful face turned fierce, her hair became a golden mane, and her teeth and nails grew long, sharp, and deadly. Before their eyes, the gentle goddess was transformed into a raging lioness.

With a fearsome roar, Hathor sprang from the palace. The men who had plotted against Ra heard her approaching and fled to the desert. In vain they tried to hide among the rocks. The raging lioness found them, every one.

> I . . . have overpowered mankind, and it was balm to my heart.
>
> ~ Hathor,
> from *The Book of the Divine Cow*

She tore them apart with her teeth and claws, and she drank their blood. Then, consumed with the ecstasy of slaughter, Hathor left the desert to ravage the towns and villages. She slew innocent men, women, and children by the thousands. Their cries rose to the heavens, and the Nile flowed red with their blood.

At last the sun set, and Hathor returned to the palace. "You have done well, Daughter," Ra praised her. "Today we prevailed over the evildoers. I have regained my power over the humans. Rest and be at peace again."

But Hathor had tasted blood and found it sweet. She was too excited to stop the slaughter. "Tomorrow I will finish the job," she vowed. "I will wade in the blood of mortals until I drink the last drop." Then the weary

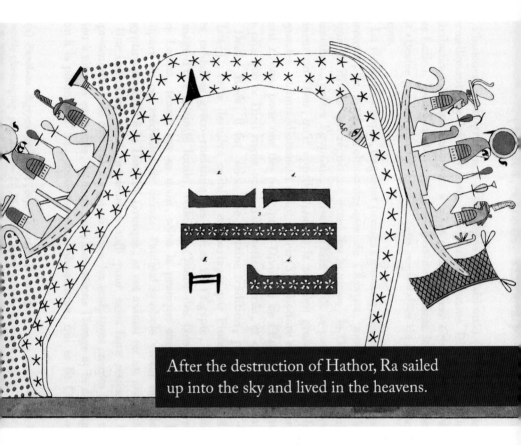

After the destruction of Hathor, Ra sailed up into the sky and lived in the heavens.

lioness curled up beside her father's throne and fell fast asleep.

That night Ra's heart was troubled. His wrath had faded, and the cries of the innocents rang in his ears. He had only meant to punish those who had defied him, not wipe out the human race completely. Hathor was out of control. How could he save the rest of humanity? At last the god came up with a plan.

Striding through the palace, Ra called for his swiftest messengers. He sent them south to the lands where the red stone called ocher is found. He commanded his high priest to grind up the ocher. He ordered his maidservants to brew large quantities of beer. The servants dyed the beer red with the ocher and filled seven thousand jars with the mixture. Just before dawn they poured the beer over the earth, flooding the fields and valleys.

Soon Hathor awoke, eager to get back to killing. She hurried from the palace and set out in search of new victims. Before long, she came to a pool of blood-red liquid that stretched as far as the eye could see. The rising sun gleamed on the surface, showing the lioness her fierce and beautiful reflection.

Hathor was delighted. How powerful she must be to have spilled so much blood! Lowering her head, she took a drink. The blood of humans tasted even better than it had the day before! Greedily the lioness lapped up the beer. As she drank, she began to grow dizzy. She forgot all about humanity. She forgot why she had ventured out into the world and what she had planned to do there. Slowly the form of the lioness faded, and Hathor stood up on two wobbly legs. With her head whirling, the goddess wandered back to the palace, where her father welcomed her warmly.

Ra sighed in relief as he restored his Eye to his forehead, but the whole episode of humankind's disobedience had left him sad and weary. Summoning the divine council once again, he announced that he no longer wished to live among mortals. At once the sky goddess Nut took the form of a cow. Ra climbed onto the back of the Divine Cow and rose up into the heavens. All the other gods and goddesses clung to the cow's belly and ascended with Ra to dwell among the stars.

After Ra had moved to the heavens, darkness covered the earth. Frightened and angry, men blamed each other for the new disaster. They took up weapons and began to fight. That is how war and misery came into the world.

Ra did not abandon the mortal world completely. With mercy, he ordered the moon god Thoth to watch over the people of Egypt. Thoth was a wise and generous guardian. He gave light to the dark night sky. He gave mortals the precious gifts of writing and knowledge. Thoth became the first of the lesser gods to take Ra's place as king on Earth.

The Origin of Day and Night

Every night, Ra was said to have battled monsters as he traveled through the underworld, fighting chaos to ensure the dawn of a new day.

A number of ancient Egyptian myths explained the daily cycle of light and darkness. According to some accounts, the sun god Ra sailed across the sky each day in his golden solar boat. When he reached the western horizon, Ra left the upper sky and steered another boat through the dark and dangerous underworld. Accompanying him on his perilous journey was a crew made up of gods, goddesses, and the spirits of dead pharaohs. The crew helped defend the sun's boat from a series of monsters. The most deadly demon was Apophis, a huge serpent that threatened to devour Ra and plunge the earth into chaos and darkness. Only after the serpent was defeated could the morning sun rise to light the world.

The nightly journey of the sun was described in an ancient text known as *The Book of the Dead*. *The Book of the Dead* was a collection of magic spells and charms that were written on **papyrus** (a type of paper made from reeds) and placed in the coffins of Egyptian nobles during the New Kingdom period. In this passage Ra's crew challenges and defeats Apophis, turning the sky from rosy dawn to the turquoise blue of full day.

"Fall back, Apophis! Enemy of Ra! Leave the edge of the sky at this voice of roaring thunder!" The gates of the horizon open for Ra to appear. He [Apophis] is helpless beneath the blows [of the gods] ...

"Bring your ropes, O Ra! that Apophis may fall to your snaring or be trapped by the gods of north, south, east and west in their traps ... The spirits of the reddening sky have trapped him. All is now well, O Ra! Proceed in peace!"

Then He [Ra] comes in his shrine; that He who set himself in motion [created himself], all alone, the unsurpassable Universal Master. And some of the gods, gathering in groups around the turquoise pools, call: "He has arisen! He has found the way! He has brought the [demons] to subjection. He has aroused the whole sky!"

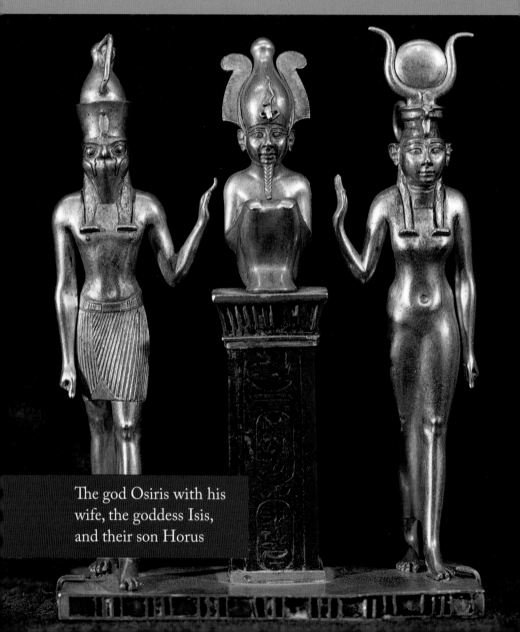

The Dying God Osiris

The god Osiris with his wife, the goddess Isis, and their son Horus

A series of gods ruled the earth after Ra withdrew to the heavens. Though none were as powerful, each had their own stories and myths of their rule. Osiris was the most important of these divine kings. He was the firstborn son of the sky goddess Nut and the earth god Geb.

Osiris was a good king who brought the arts of civilization to humankind. Under his reign Egypt enjoyed a second golden age of peace and prosperity. That perfect age came to an end when he was murdered by his evil brother, Seth. However, the story of Osiris did not end there. After his death, his grief-stricken wife searched tirelessly for his remains. Using her magical powers, Isis revived Osiris's earthly body just long enough for him to father a son and heir.

The story of Isis and Osiris explained the natural cycle of the seasons. The god's death brought the long, lifeless months of summer, when the Nile's waters receded and the blazing sun parched the land. With his revival came the season of inundation. New waters poured over the earth, and the spirit of Osiris awoke in the sprouting grain, the newborn calves, and all the other forms of rebirth and growth.

The miracle of Osiris's resurrection also gave every Egyptian hope for personal **immortality**. After conquering death, the god lived on as lord of the Afterworld. The spirits of dead mortals journeyed to Osiris's blessed domain. Those who were judged worthy were permitted to enter the Afterworld, where they enjoyed an eternity of bliss.

Many ancient Egyptian hymns, spells, and other sacred texts referred to the story of Osiris's death and resurrection. The most complete version, however, comes from a retelling by the ancient Greek historian Plutarch. Our tale is based largely on his book *Concerning Isis and Osiris*, written around 100 CE.

Dramatis Personae

Osiris (oh-SIE-rus) God of fertility, order, and the dead

Isis (EYE-sus) Goddess of nature, motherhood, and magic

Seth (SET) God of chaos, disorder, and storms

Ra (RAH) Creator and sun god

Thoth (THOATH or TOAT) God of the moon, wisdom, and writing

The Resurrection of Osiris

They say that at the hour of Osiris's birth, a voice sounded throughout the world, proclaiming, "The lord of all the earth is born!" In the course of time, the young god was hailed as king of Egypt. He took as his queen his sister Isis. For it is also said that Isis and Osiris fell in love before their birth, in the darkness of their mother's womb.

Before the reign of Osiris, the Egyptians had wandered in scattered tribes, hunting wild animals and making war against one another. The good king delivered the people from their primitive condition. He showed them how to raise crops and livestock. He gave them laws. He instructed them in the singing of hymns and other proper ways to worship the gods. Queen Isis taught women the arts of grinding grain, spinning, and weaving. She introduced the rite of marriage. So it was that under the rule of Osiris, the valley of the Nile became a rich and happy place, where all lived in truth, order, and righteousness.

After Osiris had established order in Egypt, he longed to bring his blessings to other lands. The king set out on a long journey, accompanied only by his musicians and a host of lesser gods. Wherever he traveled, he conquered the people, not with weapons but with his gentle, persuasive speech and the beauty of his songs. Soon nations far and wide rang with praises of the wise king who had brought the gifts of civilization to the whole world.

But there was one who did not praise Osiris. The king's younger brother, Seth, had a black heart filled with jealousy and wickedness. Seth longed to seize the throne of Egypt for himself. While Osiris was away, he assembled a group of greedy nobles who agreed to support his schemes. By the time the king returned to Egypt, Seth was ready with his treacherous plan.

Seth waited for a day when Isis was away from home. He invited Osiris to a banquet, along with the group of conspirators. The wicked young god had secretly obtained his brother's exact measurements and hired skilled craftsmen to make a wooden chest just that size. After the feast he brought the box into the banquet hall. All the guests gathered around to admire its fine carvings and rich decorations of gold, silver, and precious stones.

The god Seth planned to kill Osiris and take over as king.

Then Seth proposed a contest. Whoever best fit inside the box could take it home as a prize.

One by one the laughing guests tried on the cabinet for size. Some were too tall. Some were too short. Some were so thin that the box gaped around them, while others were so fat that they could not get in at all. At last it was Osiris's turn. The trusting king, whose heart was too pure to suspect anyone of evil, lay down inside the splendid cabinet. It was a perfect fit!

Osiris opened his mouth to claim his prize. But his smiles quickly turned to cries of dismay as Seth slammed down the lid, trapping him in the box. The plotters secured the lid with nails. They poured on melted lead to seal any cracks. And so the beautiful golden chest became the coffin of the king.

After Osiris had breathed his last, Seth ordered his followers to cast the heavy casket into the Nile. With the evidence of his crime safely concealed, he announced his brother's death and crowned himself king of Egypt.

Grain God

An ancient Egyptian custom honored Osiris's role as god of fertility. Each spring, as people prayed for the Nile floodwaters to bring new life to their parched land, they made a linen figure in the shape of a mummy. They stuffed the figure with wheat or barley seed and watered it. Soon seedlings began to grow from the "Grain Osiris," just as the soul of the god would come alive in the greening of the earth after the inundation.

This ancient spell from the Coffin Texts may be related to the custom of the Grain Osiris. The Coffin Texts were a body of magic spells that were carved on coffins during the Middle Kingdom period.

I am the plant of life
which comes forth from Osiris,
which grows upon the ribs of Osiris,
which allows the people to live,
which makes the gods divine,
which spiritualizes the spirits,
which sustains the masters of wealth and the masters
   of substance, ...
which enlivens the living,
which strengthens the limbs of the living.
I live as corn [grain], the life of the living.

But the box bearing the king's body did not sink into the depths of the river. Instead, it floated gently downstream to the Mediterranean Sea. The waters carried the sacred coffin all the way to the land of Byblos, in Phoenicia. There it washed ashore at the foot of a young **tamarisk** tree.

Isis was far from home when she heard the news of her husband's death. Through her magic she knew at once that Seth was behind the dreadful deed. Stricken with sorrow, the queen cut off her shining hair and donned the black garments of a widow. Then she set out in search of her husband's body.

For long days and nights, Isis wandered without sleeping, asking every man, woman, and child she met if they had seen the golden coffin. At last she came to the shores of Byblos. She sank down beside the waters, weary and dejected. Her eyes fell on the stump of a tamarisk tree. Running her fingers over the cut wood, she listened to its tale. One day, when the tree was but a sapling, the waves had laid a richly ornamented chest atop its roots. Suddenly the young tree had begun to grow with miraculous speed. As it shot skyward, it had enclosed the shining box within its massive trunk. The king of the country had marveled at the magnificent tree and ordered it cut down to make a pillar. Concealed within the mighty pillar supporting

> Osiris got into [the chest] and lay down, and those who were in the plot ran to it and slammed down the lid.
>
> ~ Plutarch, *Concerning Isis and Osiris*

Mummification And The Gods

The ancient Egyptians traced their burial practices back to the myth of Isis and Osiris. The golden chest that holds the god's body represents the coffins, often built in human shape, that the Egyptians used to protect the bodies of the dead. The goddess's steadfast search for her husband's remains reflects the belief that the body had to be preserved and given a proper burial in order for a person to be reborn in the Afterworld. Isis anoints Osiris's body with precious oils and wraps it in linen, creating the first mummy. She recites magic spells to bring the god back to life, just as the rituals performed at Egyptian funerals were believed to revive the mummified body so that part of the person's soul could live on inside it.

This hymn from the New Kingdom period praises Isis for her role in the resurrection of Osiris.

> Beneficent [kind] Isis, who rescued her brother.
> She searched for him, would not give in to her weariness,
> Wandered about this land in mourning,
> Would not take rest until she had found him.
> She shaded him with her feathers and gave him air with
>   her wings.
> She cried out for joy and brought her brother to land,
> Tempered the weakness of him who was weary of heart.
> She received his seed, giving him an heir.

the roof of the king's palace was the coffin holding the body of Osiris!

As soon as she heard the tree's story, Isis hurried to the palace. She revealed herself to the king and queen, who bowed low before the blessed goddess. Isis asked for the pillar, and her request was quickly granted. She removed the pillar from the palace with ease and cut away the wood surrounding the sacred coffin. When she opened the lid, she saw the beautiful face of Osiris, as calm and peaceful as though he were merely sleeping. Weeping bitter tears, Isis embraced her husband. Then she placed the golden box in a boat and sailed to a remote region of Lower Egypt, where she hid the coffin in the marshes.

Weary and sore at heart, Isis rested at last. While she slept, the evil king Seth chanced to go hunting by moonlight. Seth stumbled across the golden box in the marshes. Enraged at the sight of his old rival, he tore his brother's body into fourteen pieces. Then he scattered the parts all across Egypt, so that Isis could never find them all and use her magic to restore Osiris.

When Isis awoke and saw the empty coffin, she was nearly overcome with fresh sorrow. But the faithful wife was still determined to give her husband a proper funeral. Once again she began a long and patient search for Osiris's body. Wherever she found a part, she built a shrine, so that today there are many tombs of Osiris throughout Egypt. In this way the goddess tricked

> [Isis] opened the chest and laid her face upon the face within and caressed it and wept.
>
> ~ Pyramid Texts

Seth into believing that she was burying the parts of her husband's body separately.

At last Isis succeeded in recovering all the scattered remains of Osiris. Placing them in the golden casket, she anointed them with precious oils. She wrapped strips of linen around the body to hold the parts together. Then, using her powerful magic, Isis changed herself into a bird. Rising into the air, she hovered over the coffin. As she recited her magic spells, the beating of her wings fanned the breath of life into Osiris.

The god's eyes fluttered open. He gazed up at his wife tenderly. For just one night, Isis and Osiris were reunited. Through their love a child was conceived, a son named Horus who would one day avenge his father's murder.

In the morning, Osiris left the earth forever. At the command of Ra, supreme deity and god of the sun, Osiris journeyed to the Afterworld, where he would rule as king of the dead. From that time on, the people of Egypt have known that death is not an ending but a beginning. For the souls of the dead will stand before the throne of Osiris and be judged. The worthy will live forever in blessed realm of Osiris.

The Poisoning of Horus

Isis nurses her son Horus, who would grow up to rival Seth for the title of King of the World.

The myth of Horus and the scorpion is a continuation of the previous story. Osiris is dead and Isis has given birth to their child. However, she cannot bring him to the palace to claim his thrown. Instead, Isis hides the baby Horus in the marshes to protect him from Osiris's murderer, Seth. Seth knows that the child is alive and well. He becomes determined to prevent the boy from growing up and avenging his father's death. Seth hatches a plan and sends a deadly scorpion to poison Horus. Horrorstuck, Isis calls on the sun god Ra to save her child. Ra halts his solar boat and sends the moon god Thoth to save the child's life.

The story reflects the eternal battle between good and evil. If Seth succeeds in destroying the innocent child, the forces of evil and chaos will triumph. The fate of Horus is especially important because the young god is destined to become the savior of the universe. He will restore the divine order when he takes his father's place as the rightful king of Egypt.

From very early times, Egypt's mortal kings were closely identified with Horus. Every king was called not only a Son of Ra but also a living Horus. In this role, the ruler was regarded either as Horus himself, living among the people, or as a link between the human and divine worlds. The story of the baby Horus emphasized Ra's concern for his earthly "sons." Just as the great god saved Horus, he would also protect Egypt's semi-divine kings from their enemies. At the same time, it was the duty of all Egyptians to love and honor their rulers, because the divine order of the universe would collapse if the living Horus should fall.

An ancient Egyptian healing practice helped preserve the tale of Horus and the scorpion. Egyptian doctors combined the use of herbs and other practical remedies with magic spells and rituals. Their healing spells often included narratives from myths in which the gods overcame misfortunes. The following story comes from a spell against snakebite that was carved on the base of a sculpture of Horus more than two thousand years ago.

Dramatis Personae

Osiris (oh-SIE-rus) God of fertility, order, and the dead

Isis (EYE-sus) Goddess of nature, motherhood, and magic

Horus (HAWR-us) Son of Isis and Osiris; god of kingship

Seth (SET) God of chaos, disorder, and storms

Ra (RAH) Creator and sun god

Thoth (THOATH or TOAT) God of the moon, wisdom, and writing

Horus and the Scorpion

After Osiris left the earth to become king of the Afterworld, Isis fled north to the remote marshes of the Nile Delta. There the goddess gave birth to a baby boy. She named him Horus, or "He Who Is Above," because she foresaw that one day he would soar like a falcon, hunting down his enemies and restoring order to the universe. Until that day Isis kept Horus hidden from his greatest enemy, the evil king Seth.

Life was hard in the swampy Delta. To support her baby and herself, Isis was forced to disguise herself as an old woman and beg for food in the surrounding villages. Each day before she left, the goddess tucked Horus in a nest that she had made among the tall plants in a papyrus thicket.

A stele showing Horus, who is flanked by two scorpions

Back at the palace, Seth had heard rumors of Horus's birth. The treacherous king knew that he could not allow the son of Osiris to grow up and avenge his father's murder. He sent his spies to comb the land and find out where Isis and Horus were hidden. At last the divine mother and child were discovered in the Delta. When Seth heard the news, he sat on his throne, brooding. He did not dare enter the marshes and attack the boy personally, for fear of the prophecies that said Horus would one day overthrow him. So his evil mind devised a cruel plan. He would send his spirit in the form of a scorpion to poison the innocent child.

The following day, Isis returned from begging, eager to embrace her little son. But when she parted the tall plants and peered into the nest, she found Horus limp and lifeless. There were tears on his cheeks and foam on his lips. She laid her head on his chest. His heart was barely beating.

At once, the horrified mother suspected that Seth had caused her son's illness. Without knowing what he had done to injure Horus, however, she could not use her magic to heal the baby. Never had Isis felt so alone. "Who will come if I call for help?" she lamented. "My husband is dead. My father and mother are too far away to hear my pleas. My brother Seth is my constant enemy. Oh, who will help my innocent child, my beautiful golden Horus?"

Suddenly Isis remembered the men and women of the marshes. She cried out, and the people came running. Everyone wept over the suffering child, but no one knew how to cure him. One of the fishermen ran to fetch a healer who was visiting his village. The woman took the infant in her arms. "Do not fear, little Horus," she murmured. "Do not despair, mother of the god. Seth does not dare enter this region. He must have sent a snake or scorpion to bite Horus."

Quickly Isis examined her son. The wise woman was right. Horus had been poisoned. In the wildness of her despair, Isis lifted her head and howled to the heavens. "Oh Ra! Horus has been bitten! Horus, the lonely, unprotected child. Horus, who must grow to avenge his father. Horus, son of your son, heir of your heir, link between your kingship and the world of mortals!"

Carried by the strength of her magic, the goddess's cries reached the solar boat as it passed above in the heavens. Quickly Ra brought the boat to a halt, plunging the earth into darkness. Then he sent down his deputy Thoth, armed with the power and authority to put things right again.

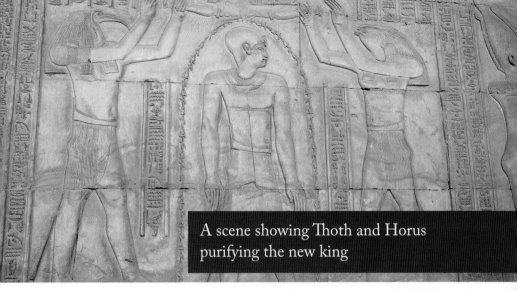

A scene showing Thoth and Horus purifying the new king

"What is the trouble, Isis?" Thoth called as he alighted in the marshes. "Surely nothing can have happened to Horus that you cannot heal with your powerful magic. Ra has pledged that the solar boat will not start again until the child recovers."

"Disaster upon disaster!" cried Isis. "My son has been poisoned. Seth has sent a scorpion to inflict the deadly illness. If Horus dies and the sun ceases its journey, all creation will be shattered. How I wish that I had died with Osiris so that I need never have seen such suffering!"

"Fear not, divine mother," Thoth soothed the grieving goddess. "Ra has sent me with the breath of life to cure Horus. From this day onward, your son will be as safe as the sun itself when it lights up the world with its splendor."

Then Thoth turned to the stricken child and uttered his magic spells: "Awake, Horus! The great god Ra himself is your protection. Out, poison! Ra himself commands you. The boat of the sun will stand still until Horus recovers. Darkness will cover the world. The wells will dry, the crops will wither, and humankind will starve for vegetation.

Out, poison, so that the light of the sun can resume its journey and fill every heart with rejoicing."

The little boy stirred in his mother's arms. He opened his eyes and began to cry for his supper. "The poison is dead!" proclaimed Thoth. "Horus lives again, to the delight of Isis!"

At that, all the marsh dwellers rejoiced. Observing their devotion, Thoth entrusted Horus to their care. He commanded them to watch over the divine child, protecting and serving him until he was old enough to claim the throne of his father. Ra himself would guard Horus from above, while Isis would use her magic powers to make sure all the people of Egypt loved and honored him.

After this final proclamation, Thoth returned to the sky. He came to Ra and informed him that Horus was alive and well. There was great joy aboard the solar boat as it set sail once again, ending the darkness. As life returned to normal Isis sat in the marshes, nursing her son.

The Seven Scorpions of Isis

Magic was part of everyday life in ancient Egypt. Priests, scribes, and healers used magic spells, magic wands, and other supernatural means to help people get what they desired, from love and health to a new baby or a successful harvest. Magic was also used to prevent or cure common perils such as illness, pain, and snake or scorpion bites.

No Egyptian deity was believed to have greater magical powers than Isis. In "The Poisoning of Horus," Isis calls on Ra to heal her son, but in many other myths, she demonstrates her own healing powers. In a story known as "Isis and the Seven Scorpions," the goddess is accompanied by seven scorpions as she flees from her evil brother Seth. Disguised as a beggar, she calls on a wealthy noblewoman, who slams the door in her face. Angered by such inhospitable behavior, a scorpion named Tefen stings the noblewoman's baby son. In this passage from an ancient spell against snakebite, Isis describes how she took pity on the dying infant.

At this point my heart misgave me about the little child. I wanted to cure him—for he, after all, was quite innocent. So I cried out to her [the mother] saying: "Come to me! Come to me who have the secret of life. I am a 'daughter' [healer], one well known in her town, who can expel poison with her spell ..."

So Isis laid her hands on the child to soothe him as he lay panting for breath. "O Poison of Tefen, come, flow to the ground! ... May the child live and the poison die ..."

It was as if the fire had been extinguished and the sky calmed down through the spell of the divine Isis. Then the rich lady went and brought her possessions out of her own house ... She would be ready to give away all her possessions if she could undo the results of her not opening her door to me.

The Quarrel of Horus and Seth

Horus smites Seth, who is represented here as a donkey. The two fought for centuries before there was a victor.

When Seth ruled the mortal world, Egypt was plagued with violence and disorder. The people of Egypt had to wait until Horus grew old enough to challenge his uncle for the throne. Finally, Horus challenged his uncle. The battle raged for hundreds of years. As the fighting continued, the other gods grew weary of the disturbance. At last, they called a great council to decide who should rule the earth.

Some gods believed Seth should rule, because he was older and stronger. Others argued that Horus was the rightful heir to his father's throne. Finally, Isis came up with a clever trick that convinced the divine court to proclaim her son king of Egypt.

This ancient myth was a powerful validation of Egypt's system of dynastic rule. Horus, the son and rightful heir of Osiris, represents the forces of divine order. Seth, who has seized the throne by force, stands for darkness, destruction, and chaos. Horus's triumph over Seth restores order to the universe. In the same way, Egypt would enjoy peace and prosperity as long as the king's son and rightful heir sat on the throne.

After Horus wins the throne, he journeys to the Afterworld to give his father the good news. Every newly crowned king of Egypt followed the god's example in a series of rituals performed during the dead king's funeral. Even when a king died without having fathered any children, these ancient rites confirmed that his successor was the true "son" and heir. The rituals also allowed the dead king to become one with Osiris, ensuring that the powers of life and growth would continue to bless the land.

The story of the divine battle for Egypt's throne is found in many ancient texts, including hymns, spells, and books of rituals written on papyrus or carved in stone. During the New Kingdom, an unknown scribe produced a long, sometimes comical account known as *The Contendings of Horus and Seth*. The Greek historian Plutarch also told his own version of the tale. The story that follows is a blending of several of these ancient sources.

Dramatis Personae

Seth (SET) God of chaos, disorder, and storms

Osiris (oh-SIE-rus) God of fertility, order, and the dead

Isis (EYE-sus) Goddess of nature, motherhood, and magic

Horus (HAWR-us) Son of Isis and Osiris; god of kingship

Ra (RAH) Creator and sun god

Thoth (THOATH or TOAT) God of the moon, wisdom, and writing

Shu (SHOO) God of the air

Seth, Horus, and the Trickery of Isis

When Seth sat on the throne of Osiris, darkness and disorder reigned in Egypt. Innocent men and women were murdered or robbed. Followers of the true king were driven from their homes. To escape the persecution, people fled to the remote regions of the Nile Delta.

Among the fugitives were Osiris's wife, Isis, and their young son, Horus.

As soon as Horus grew to manhood, his mother sat him down and told him the story of his father's murder. She told him how his wicked uncle had conspired to steal the kingship. The proud young god listened in silence. Then he made a solemn vow to overthrow the false king Seth and reclaim the throne of his father.

Horus gathered together the scattered supporters of Osiris. He led his army out of the Delta to wage war on Seth's forces. The battle between the two gods was long and bitter, with much death and destruction on each side. In fact, the quarrel became so fierce that the entire universe trembled. Up in the heavens, Ra called for his deputy, Thoth. "What is going on down in the world of humans?" the great god exclaimed. "Seth and Horus have stirred up so much strife that the earth is brown and trampled. You must call a council and decide which of those two fools is the rightful heir, before they destroy everything that I created."

So Thoth summoned the gods and goddesses to Ra's temple at Heliopolis. Horus was the first to appear before the divine council. The youngster presented a passionate argument, claiming that only the son of the king had the right to inherit the throne. Then it was Seth's turn. The villainous god sneered at Horus's claim. "I am older and stronger than that puny pretender," Seth boasted. "I alone have the strength to defend Egypt from its enemies."

After the two opponents had spoken, the council debated. Most of the members were convinced that Horus was the rightful heir. "Justice should prevail over

The Eyes of Horus

Horus was often pictured as a divine falcon whose right eye was the sun and left eye was the moon. In some accounts of the great quarrel between Seth and Horus, the older god rips out his nephew's left eye and hides or destroys it. The god Thoth soon recovers the eye and restores Horus's sight. To the ancient Egyptians, this mythological event explained the cycles of the moon.

The Contendings of Horus and Seth gives a slightly different version of the incident. Here Horus loses both of his eyes but is miraculously healed by the goddess Hathor.

[Seth] threw [Horus] on his back on the ground and tore his two eyes from their sockets and buried them on the mountainside. And there the two eyeballs became two flower buds which grew into lotus flowers which light up the earth ...

Then Hathor ... went and found Horus lying weeping on the mountainside. She took a gazelle, milked it, and addressed Horus. "Open your eyes that I may rub in these drops of milk." She did this in the right and in the left eye. "Open your eyes," she said to him. He did so. She looked upon him and found that all was well again.

sheer strength," declared Shu, god of the air. "We should award the throne to the son of Osiris."

"Right! A million times right!" proclaimed Thoth. "Let us present the crown to Horus, since that is the court's judgment."

"Not so fast!" bellowed Ra. "What do you mean by issuing a judgment without hearing my opinion?" Then, because he was so annoyed with the council, the great god took Seth's side in the quarrel. "Horus is a mere lad, too young and weak to rule," he said. "The throne should go to the boy's uncle, for his strength is greater."

At that, the argument really grew heated. Some of the gods argued for the rights of Horus. Others raised their voices to praise the might of Seth. Isis, who had been smoldering in silence throughout the debate, finally lost her patience. "How can a court of gods commit such wrongs!" she shouted. "You had better give the throne to Horus, before the sky crashes to the earth in anger!"

More than one god cast a nervous eye toward the heavens. Speaking soothingly, they tried to calm Isis by promising that her son would receive justice. Then it was Seth's turn to get angry. Rattling his royal **scepter**, he vowed, "I will have nothing more to do with this court as long as Isis is a member."

Ra, who was growing weary of the endless arguments, called for silence. Hoping to restore the peace, he ordered a change of scene. The council would move to an island in the middle of the Nile River. Just to make sure there were no more interruptions, the great god gave a command to the ferryman: "Do not ferry over any women, especially not one who looks like Isis."

So the council crossed over to the island and sat down to a feast in a grand pavilion. But it seems they'd forgotten about Isis's magical powers. In a blink the determined goddess transformed herself into a haggard old woman. Groaning and muttering, she hobbled up to the riverbank.

"Carry me across to the island, good ferryman," she said. "I must take a loaf of barley bread to the boy who tends the cattle."

"I was ordered not to transport any woman who might be Isis," the man protested.

"Do I look like a radiant goddess?" croaked the old hag. "Come, I will give you this nice bread if you take me to the island."

"What do I want with that moldy loaf!" exclaimed the man. "Should I disobey orders for a loaf of barley bread?"

"Well then, I will give you this golden ring from my finger."

One look at the fine ring and the ferryman consented. He brought Isis to the island, then hurried back across the waters. As soon as she stepped ashore, the goddess whispered another magic spell and transformed herself into a lovely young woman. Seth was dining among the gods when he saw her approaching. Captivated by her beauty, he hurried over to greet her.

> Shall one give the cattle to the stranger, while the son of the owner is still here?
>
> ~ *The Contendings of Horus and Seth*

"How can I help you, my pretty?" asked the god.

"Oh great lord! I have come seeking justice," cried the disguised goddess. "I am a poor widow. I was married to a cowherd and bore him a son. When my husband died, the boy looked after his father's herd. Then a stranger came to our home. He threatened to beat my young son and claim the cattle for himself. Will you help my son recover his inheritance?"

Seth puffed up with outrage. "Indeed I will," he said. "A stranger has no right to take a man's property when the son and heir is living."

The moment she heard those words, Isis changed herself into a bird. She flew to the top of a tree, safely out of Seth's reach. Then she called down mockingly, "Your own mouth betrays you, wretched thief! Your own verdict condemns you!"

Seth realized that he had been tricked. Weeping tears of rage, he rushed over to the council and complained about the goddess's deception. When Ra heard that Seth had defended the son's right to his inheritance, he pronounced his final judgment. Horus was the true heir to the throne of Osiris.

On the day that Horus was crowned king of Egypt, the people rejoiced. The long quarrel between the gods was over, and the world was at peace again. As his first act, the new king journeyed to the Afterworld, where his father lay sleeping. He embraced Osiris and gave him the glad news of his coronation. Then all the earth awoke, and the world became new and green and fruitful again.

As for Seth, evil though he was, he finally accepted the judgment of the court, and honored Horus as the master of all lands for all eternity. Then Ra in his wisdom took his defeated son to dwell with him in the sky, as the god of storms. Every night Seth journeys with Ra through the dark underworld, defending the solar boat against the dangerous serpent Apophis. Seth protects the sun and provides the balance he always sought to disrupt. Yet Seth still has a powerful presence in this world. When the lord of storms raises his voice, the earth trembles with the sound of thunder.

The fact that Osiris ruled in the Afterworld gave the ancient Egyptians hope, both for this world and the next one. Each year the god would awaken to bless the land of Egypt with new life. And when a person died, Osiris would help his or her ba (soul) gain eternal life.

Before the ba could enter the Afterworld, it faced judgment before the throne of Osiris. A court of forty-two divine judges helped the god determine whether the dead person had lived a good life. The jackal-headed god Anubis had an especially important role. He placed the person's heart on a set of scales and weighed it against the feather of Maat, goddess of truth, justice, and order. If the heart balanced against the feather,

The head of the god Osiris, king of the Afterworld

the ba was admitted to Osiris's domain. If the heart was heavy with sin, it was devoured by a hungry monster, and the person ceased to exist.

The Book of the Dead offered detailed instructions on what a person should say and do during the journey to the Afterworld. The following passage is entitled "What is to be said when one reaches the Hall of Truth."

Homage [praise] to you, Great God, the Lord of the double
  Ma'at [Truth]!
I have come to you, my Lord,
I have brought myself here to behold your beauties.
I know you, and I know your name,
And I know the names of the two and forty gods
Who live with you in the Hall of the Two Truths,
Who imprison the sinners, and feed upon their blood,
in the day when the lives of men are judged in the presence of
  Osiris ...
Grant that I may come to you,
For I have committed no faults,
I have not sinned,
I have not done evil,
I have not lied,
Therefore let nothing evil happen to me.
I live on maat, and I feed on maat,
I have performed the commandments of maat and the things
  pleasing to the gods ...
Deliver me, protect me, accuse me not in the presence of Osiris.
I am pure of mouth and pure of hands,
Therefore, let all who see me welcome me.

The Birth of a Great King

This is a sculpture of the female King Hatshepsut. She is even given a beard here, to present herself as undisputed king.

Becaused they Egyptian myths said that rulers were decendents of the gods, even real-life kings were surrounded by myth and mystery. As a descendent of Ra, the king was believed to carry out the creator god's plans for the universe. As a living Horus, the ruler fulfilled the judgment of the divine court that awarded the throne to Horus, son of Osiris.

What happened when the "son" was a "daughter"? Sources tell us that nearly all of Egypt's kings were men. However several women became well known as powerful pharaohs. One of the most remarkable of these female pharaohs was Hatshepsut.

Hatshepsut was the daughter of the New Kingdom pharaoh Thutmose I. After her father's death, she married her half brother, who ruled Egypt as Thutmose II. The new pharaoh died without leaving a male heir, except for the infant son of one of his "lesser" wives. Hatshepsut was appointed regent, or temporary ruler, until the future Thutmose III was old enough to take command. The queen soon broke with tradition, however, and declared herself king.

The new king justified her actions by claiming that she was the daughter of Amun-Ra, the most important god of the New Kingdom period. Images and texts carved on the walls of Hatshepsut's temples explained her miraculous birth. The story told through the inscriptions established this "female Horus" as the rightful heir to the throne.

Hatshepsut ruled for about twenty years. When she died, Thutmose III finally became king. Toward the end of his life, Thutmose tried to wipe out all traces of his powerful stepmother, perhaps to ensure his own son's peaceful succession. Statues of Hatshepsut were destroyed, and the inscriptions were carefully chiseled away from her temple walls. Despite these efforts, in the temple of Deir el-Bahri, in ancient Thebes (modern-day Luxor), a "shadow" of the lost images remained. Historians have pieced together the myth of Hatshepsut's divine birth from this ancient story carved in stone.

Dramatis Personae

Amun-Ra (AH-mun RAH) Creator and sun god during New Kingdom period

Thutmose I (thoot-MOH-suh) Eighteenth Dynasty king of Egypt

Thoth (THOATH or TOAT) God of the moon, wisdom, and writing

Ahmose (ah-MOH-suh) Wife and queen of Thutmose

Hatshepsut (hat-SHEP-soot) Daughter of Thutmose; Eighteenth Dynasty ruler

Khnum (KUH-num) Ram-headed potter god

The Miraculous Birth of Hatshepsut

In the land of the gods, Amun-Ra sat on his throne and pondered a weighty question. As father of the world and all its creatures, the great god had a special interest in the throne of Egypt. The present pharaoh, Thutmose, was a good ruler. But even a king who was both human and divine could not live forever. Who would reign over Egypt when Thutmose died and took his place among the gods?

Suddenly Amun-Ra had a brilliant idea. Summoning his council of gods and goddesses, he let them in on his plan. "It is time for the world to have a female pharaoh," he announced, "so that people will not forget to honor the strength and wisdom of women. I will personally place a part of myself inside the new king, so that my spirit may guide her as she rules."

All of the council members (especially the goddesses) applauded Amun-Ra's plan. Thoth, god of wisdom, added his own clever counsel. "In the royal palace at Thebes," he said, "there dwells the most beautiful woman in the world. She is Ahmose, wife of Thutmose, king of Egypt. Let her be the mother of the new pharaoh."

"So be it," said Amun-Ra. And that very night, Thoth changed himself into his favorite form, an ibis. The swift-flying bird led the king of gods to the royal palace. There Amun-Ra took on the outer form of the pharaoh, so that he could slip past the queen's guards and maidservants. He entered Ahmose's bedchamber. He gazed down on her as she lay sleeping in the moonlight.

> Amun Ra took the form of the noble King Thutmose and found the queen sleeping in her room.
>
> ~ Inscription from Hatshepsut's temple

He breathed divine life into her nostrils, and the room filled with the scent of the gods, sweeter than the richest perfumes. The beautiful woman awakened. Before her stood Amun-Ra, bathed in a golden light, wearing his double-plumed crown and the precious gold collar of the pharaohs.

A wall painting of the
ram-headed god Khnum

"Do not fear, fairest queen," said the god gently.
"You will give birth to a daughter, and you will name her
Hatshepsut ('Foremost of the Noble'), because she carries
my divine spark within her. She will rule over Egypt under
my guidance and protection."

Then Amun-Ra left the palace and went straight to
Khnum, the ram-headed god who had been entrusted

Gods of Childbirth

The myth of the divine birth of Hatshepsut features a few of the many Egyptian deities especially associated with women. Hathor, who ravaged humankind in our earlier story "Ra's Wrath," appears in her more common role as a goddess of motherhood and childbirth. Bes, a fierce-looking but good-natured dwarf, was believed to protect women in labor and guard children from snakes and scorpions. Meskhenet determined the destiny of every newborn. The frog goddess Heket assisted in childbirth. The kindly hippopotamus goddess Taweret watched over pregnant women and young children.

The ancient Egyptians used prayers, magic spells, and amulets to call on these special deities and seek their protection for mothers-to-be and infants. Spells to ease childbirth often identified the mother with Isis and the baby with Horus. The following spell was recited four times over a clay amulet of Bes, which was placed on the brow of the woman in labor:

> O good dwarf, come, because of the one who sent you ...
> I am Horus who conjures [summons] in order that she who is giving birth becomes better than she was, as if she was already delivered ... Look, Hathor will lay her hand on her with an amulet of health! I am Horus who saves her!

with the making of the first man and woman. "We must prepare for the birth of my daughter Hatshepsut," said the king of gods. "Fashion two figures, one for her human body and one for her immortal ka. Take care to make them even better than the gods, for she will be a great king who will rule Egypt with honor and glory all the days of her life."

Khnum bowed his massive ram head. Sitting down at his potter's wheel, he went straight to work making the body and spirit of Amun-Ra's divine daughter. As his able hands shaped the clay, he muttered powerful incantations. He gave the figures long life and strength, riches and happiness. He endowed them with unearthly beauty, so that they would shine like the sun upon the throne of Horus.

When Khnum had finished his task, the divine council came to admire Amun-Ra's daughter. They carried the figures to a special chamber that had been prepared in the palace of Thutmose. Then they led Queen Ahmose to the birthing chamber.

All the special deities who watch over mothers and newborn babies gathered for the birth of Hatshepsut. The great mother Isis and Ra's daughter Hathor were there. So was ugly little Bes, protector of young children. Also in the company were the hippopotamus goddess Taweret, the frog goddess Heket, and Meskhenet, goddess of childbirth and destiny. With so much divine help, the queen had no trouble delivering her child. Soon she was cradling little Hatshepsut in her arms. All the attendants marveled at the child's beauty and chanted praises in her name.

At the height of this celebration, the doors of the chamber opened. In walked Amun-Ra himself. Taking his newborn daughter in his arms, he welcomed her to the world:. "Welcome, Hatshepsut. Welcome, future king. I grant you my fame and power. May you reign in peace and prosperity …"

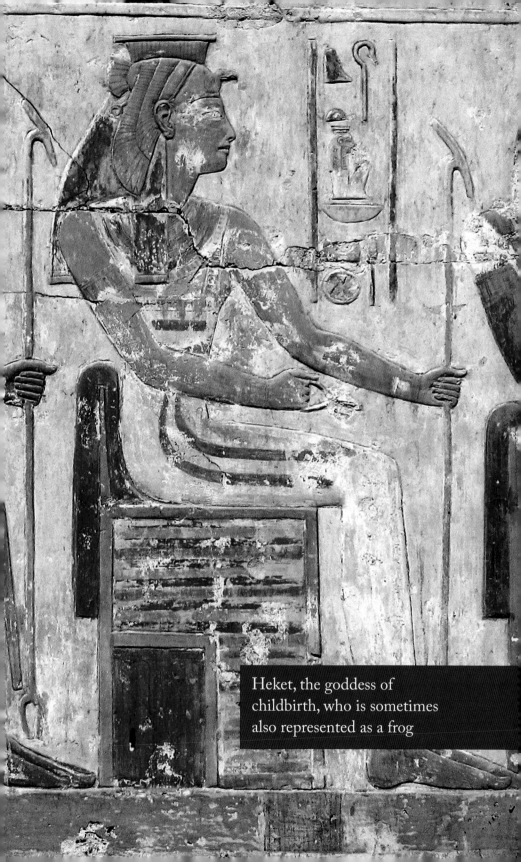

Heket, the goddess of childbirth, who is sometimes also represented as a frog

GLOSSARY

amulets	Small images of gods, goddesses, animals, hieroglyphs, and other beings or objects, which were worn or carried for good luck and protection.
ba	The part of the soul that represented an individual's personality or identity. After death the ba made a perilous journey to the Afterworld.
hieroglyphs	The ancient Egyptian writing system, which used pictures and symbols that stood for words and sounds.
immortality	The state of being immortal, or living forever.
inscriptions	Words engraved in stone or some other hard surface.
inundation	The annual flooding of the Nile River.
ka	The part of the soul that represented a person's spiritual double or life force. After death the ka continued to dwell in the preserved body.

lapis lazuli	A deep blue stone used in ancient Egyptian jewelry and other treasures.
maat	The divine order of the universe, which was decreed by the gods. The word maat can also mean "truth," "justice," "righteousness," and "balance."
mummification	The process of preserving a body as a mummy.
papyrus	A type of paper made from reeds that grew along the banks of the Nile.
pharaoh	A king of ancient Egypt.
primeval	Original; existing from earliest times.
scepter	A staff carried by a king as a symbol of authority.
scribes	Educated Egyptians who kept official records, wrote personal letters, and performed other writing jobs for a living.
silt	Small particles of earth deposited by water.
tamarisk	A desert tree or shrub with long feathery branches.
vizier	A civil officer in Egypt, a very important official.

ANCIENT TEXTS OF THE EGYPTIAN MYTHS

Like other ancient peoples, the Egyptians passed down their myths orally for centuries. Many of their traditional tales have probably been lost forever. Those that have survived were written down on papyrus scrolls or inscribed or painted on coffins, sculptures, and the walls of tombs and temples. These ancient texts rarely tell a story from beginning to end. Instead, scholars have pieced together the myths from bits and pieces found in many different sources. The ancient Greeks also retold a number of Egyptian myths, preserving tales that might otherwise have been lost.

The stories in this book are based mainly on the following ancient Egyptian sources:

The Pyramid Texts

The Pyramid Texts are the oldest surviving collection of Egyptian funerary literature (writings associated with burials). They include a total of about eight hundred spells, charms, hymns, prayers, offerings, and other sacred texts, which were carved inside the pyramid tombs of kings and queens late in the Old Kingdom period and in the First Intermediate period. No two pyramids had the same number or combination of inscriptions.

The Coffin Texts

The Coffin Texts are a group of more than one thousand religious spells and prayers from the Middle Kingdom period. These ancient texts were carved mainly on the inside walls of wooden coffins to help the spirits of the dead find their way to the Afterworld. Some of the spells were illustrated with maps to guide the dead during their difficult journey.

The Book of the Dead

The Book of the Dead is our modern name for a collection of nearly two hundred magic spells and charms that was known to the ancient Egyptians as *The Book of Going Forth by Day*. Beginning in the New Kingdom period, the spells were written on papyrus scrolls and placed in special containers in the coffins of wealthy Egyptians. These sacred texts were believed to aid and protect the spirits of the dead on their journey to the Afterworld.

The Book of the Divine Cow

The Book of the Divine Cow was a collection of magic spells carved in the tombs of several pharaohs during the New Kingdom period. It consisted mainly of an account of the sun god Ra's rule on earth following creation. The spells were intended to identify the dead king with Ra, in order to help the king's spirit rise to the heavens. The earliest known version of *The Book of the Divine Cow* was inscribed in a golden shrine containing the coffin of Tutankhamen, who ruled Egypt from about 1361 to 1352 BCE.

The Contendings of Horus and Seth

Sometime during the New Kingdom period, an unknown scribe drew from a variety of sources to write this lengthy account of the battle between the gods Seth and Horus for the throne of Egypt. Unlike the mostly solemn and reverent religious texts of ancient Egypt, this unusual story pokes fun at the gods and goddesses.

THE LIVING MYTHS

The ancient Egyptians had a deep and lasting influence on their neighbors, trading partners, and even their enemies. The ancient Greeks and Romans admired and imitated the Egyptian civilization. Nations as far east as Persia (modern-day Iran) and as far west as Britain adopted parts of Egyptian mythology into their own cultures. Today that ancient legacy continues to inspire wonder and imagination. You can see it in the Eye of Ra that peers out from a pyramid on the back of the US dollar bill. You can experience it in modern stories depicting the phoenix, the sphinx, and other Egyptian mythological beings. Here are a few of the many other areas in which the ancient Egyptians have touched our modern world.

Books

Inside the Illusion (Everworld series, K. A. Applegate)

The Oracle Betrayed (The Oracle Prophecies Series, Catherine Fisher)

Ramses series (Christian Jacq)

Stargate series (Bill McCay)

The Kane Chronicle series (Rick Riordan)

The Egypt Game (Zilpha Keatley Snyder)

Film

Stargate (1994)

The Mummy (1999)

The Mummy Returns (2001)

The Scorpion King (2002)

Television Series

Stargate SG-1

Tutenstein

The Young Indiana Jones Chronicles

Books

Ashworth, Leon. *Gods and Goddesses of Ancient Egypt.* North Mankato, MN: Smart Apple Media, 2003.

Gahlin, Lucia. *Egypt: Gods, Myths and Religion.* New York: Barnes and Noble Books, 2002.

Hinds, Kathryn. *Life in Ancient Egypt.* New York: Marshall Cavendish Benchmark, 2007.

Malam, John. *Myths and Legends of the Desert.* New York: Kingfisher, 2002.

Marston, Elsa. *The Ancient Egyptians.* New York: Benchmark Books, 1996.

Nardo, Don. *Egyptian Mythology.* Berkeley Heights, NJ: Enslow, 2001.

Parker, Vic. *Traditional Tales from Ancient Egypt.* North Mankato, MN: Thameside Press, 2000.

Pinch, Geraldine. *Handbook of Egyptian Mythology.* Santa Barbara, CA: ABC-CLIO, 2002.

Quie, Sarah. *Myths and Civilization of the Ancient Egyptians.* New York: Peter Bedrick, 1998.

Remler, Pat. *Egyptian Mythology A to Z.* New York: Facts on File, 2000.

Storm, Rachel. *Mythology of Egypt and the Middle East.* London: Southwater, 2003.

Websites

The Book of the Dead

www.sacred-texts.com/egy/ebod

The Book of the Dead is one of the most important surviving sources of Egyptian mythology. This electronic edition is based on the translation by E. A. Wallis Budge.

Mummy Secrets—Unwrapped!

www.lsa.umich.edu/lsa/ci.mummysecrets unwrapped_ci.detail

This site from the University of Michigan is packed with information on the steps involved with mummification. Click on "All about the Afterlife" to explore Egyptian beliefs about resurrection and life after death.

Mysteries of Egypt

www.civilization.ca/civil/egypt/egcivile.html

The Canadian Museum of Civilization presents this informative introduction to the geography, government, arts and sciences, daily life, writings, and religion of the ancient Egyptians. Click on "Religion" for information on beliefs, practices, and myths.

Odyssey Online: Egypt

www.carlos.emory.edu/ODYSSEY/EGYPT/homepg.html

Read or listen to a version of an Egyptian creation story at this Emory University site. You'll also find a variety of interactive games and information on daily life, death, burial, and lots more.

Ten Facts About Ancient Egypt

www.ngkids.co.uk/history/ten-facts-about-ancient-egypt#

Check out this website for interesting facts about ancient Egypt. Check out the links that describe different Egyptian gods and learn some hieroglyphics! Part of National Geographic Kids, the site is full of exciting tidbits.

Bulfinch, Thomas. *The Golden Age of Myth and Legend.* Hertfordshire, England: Wordsworth Reference, 1993.

Clark, R. T. Rundle. *Myth and Symbol in Ancient Egypt.* New York: Thames and Hudson, 1959.

Fleming, Fergus, and Alan Lothian. *The Way to Eternity: Egyptian Myth.* Time-Life Books, 1997.

Freeman, Charles. *The Legacy of Ancient Egypt.* New York: Facts on File, 1997.

Hart, George. *Egyptian Myths.* Austin: University of Texas Press, 1992.

James, T. G. H. *Myths and Legends of Ancient Egypt.* New York: Grosset and Dunlap, 1971.

Mackenzie, Donald A. *Egyptian Myths and Legends.* New York: Gramercy, 1994.

Redford, Donald B., ed. *The Ancient Gods Speak: A Guide to Egyptian Religion.* New York: Oxford University Press, 2002.

Spence, Lewis. *Ancient Egyptian Myths and Legends.* New York: Dover, 1990.

Wilkinson, Richard H. *The Complete Gods and Goddesses of Ancient Egypt.* London: Thames and Hudson, 2003.

Quoted passages in sidebars come from the following sources:

The passage from *The Book of the Dead* in "The Origin of Day and Night" page 46; the spell from the Coffin Texts in "Grain God," page 53; the hymn to Isis in "Mummification and the Gods," page 55; the spell against snakebite in "The Seven Scorpions of Isis," page 65; and the passage from *The Contendings of Horus and Seth* in "The Eyes of Horus," page 70, from R. T. Rundle Clark, *Myth and Symbol in Ancient Egypt* (New York: Thames and Hudson, 1959).

The passage from *The Book of the Dead* in "Judgment in the Afterlife," page 74, translated by Richard Hooker, at http://www.wsu.edu/~dee/EGYPT/BOD125.HTM

INDEX

Page numbers in **boldface** are illustrations. Entries in **boldface** are glossary terms.